THE FACES OF WORLD WAR II

MAX HASTINGS

WITH CAPTIONS AND PICTURE SELECTION BY MICHAEL WALSH

MAX HASTINGS

THE FACES OF
WORLD WAR II

CASSELL
ILLUSTRATED

Previous page **WEARY TROOPS** *prepare for their evacuation from Dunkirk.*

Right **AMERICAN TROOPS** *on board a landing craft heading for Oran, Algeria, November 1942.*

First published in Great Britain in 2008 by Cassell Illustrated, an imprint of Octopus Publishing Group Limited, 2–4 Heron Quays, London E14 4JP.

Copyright © Octopus Publishing Group 2008
Text copyright © Max Hastings

A CIP catalogue record for this book is available from the British Library.

ISBN-13: 978 1 844 03626 4

Distributed in the United States and Canada by Sterling Publishing Co., Inc
387 Park Avenue South, New York, NY 10016-8810

10 9 8 7 6 5 4 3 2

Printed and bound in China

contents

Author's Introduction [6]

PRE-WAR *Rise of Nazism—Germany annexes Czechoslovakia* [10]

1939 *Germany invades Poland— Winter War* [22]

1940 *Churchill appointed Prime Minister—Operation Compass* [46]

1941 *War in the Mediterranean—Japan attacks Pearl Harbor* [84]

1942 *Singapore falls to Japan—Battle of Stalingrad* [122]

1943 *German defeat at Stalingrad— US "island-hopping" campaign* [162]

1944 *Monte Cassino—Battle of the Bulge* [198]

1945 *Iwo-Jima—surrender of Japan* [238]

POSTWAR [272]

index [284]

acknowledgements [288]

introduction

AT THE OUTBREAK of World War II, photography as an art was already a century old. The *New York Daily Graphic* published the first newspaper photograph in 1880. Britain's *Daily Mirror* became the first paper to adopt all-photographic illustration in 1904. Images of battlefields were created for posterity as early as the Crimea in 1854. Thereafter, pictures were taken during the American Civil War, the Boer War, and many lesser conflicts. A host of photos survive from World War I. Yet until the 1930s technology, which demanded big, heavy, tripod-mounted cameras and long exposures, made it almost impossible to capture combat. Virtually all photographs emanating from war zones depicted static scenes of people and places. Most shots which purported to show men in battle were, in reality, taken in training or behind the front line.

All this changed dramatically in the decade before Hitler's war. The introduction of highly portable 35-mm cameras, most famously the German Leica, created a new genre of actuality photography, showcased in such magazines as the British *Picture Post* and the American *Life*, the German *Berliner Illustrietre* and *Munchener Illustrietre*. Photographers willing to risk their lives began to record remarkable images on the world's battle-fields, such as Robert Capa's picture of a Republican

soldier at the moment of his death, from the Spanish Civil War. The Hungarian-born Capa, twenty-five in 1938, was already celebrated that year by *Picture Post* as "the greatest war photographer in the world". Yet he preferred to describe himself as a journalist, seeking "the decisive moment... I'd rather have a strong image that is technically bad than vice versa", he said.

When World War II began, every combatant country possessed young men, and a few young women, with skills, courage and equipment to tell the story of the greatest conflict in history in pictures, in a fashion hitherto impossible. The Nazis, under the direction of supreme propagandist Dr. Josef Goebbels, inevitably set about the business on the most ambitious scale. "Photo reporters" were trained at the Alexander Barracks in Berlin. They were taught, for instance, that battle pictures must always be taken from elevated positions "because the German soldier stands tall and is in command of events". They were instructed to photograph as many enemy dead as possible, but no German corpses. They learned always to depict Hitler's troops advancing from left to right – eastwards, in the direction of Poland and Russia. Then they were drafted to Propaganda Companies 250 strong, each with 120 vehicles and motorcycle messengers to rush film to the nearest airfield, and deployed among the armies. By 1943, more than 15,000 reporters and cameramen were serving with Germany's armed forces.

German photographers received only army pay, but newspapers and magazines such as *Signal* and *Der Adler* paid one mark for each image used, allegedly towards a fund for the war disabled. By the time of Hitler's invasion of Russia in June 1941, the advancing panzers were accompanied by a "photograph train" which included a fourteen-ton portable darkroom. One camera was equipped with a zoom lens more than a yard long. Every image was to be exploited for the service of Nazi Germany, and was thus framed accordingly. "Photos of prisoners", ordered Goebbels on May 29, 1940, "should only be used when they give an impression of being thoroughly cowed". The following year, propaganda companies accompanying the invasion of Greece were told: "photographs of German troops being greeted joyfully by the populace of Salonika are to be provided". During the Eastern campaign, German pictures of Russian imperial furniture at Gashina Castle near Leningrad were censored, because some pieces bore images of copulating couples. The Nazis' cameramen often recorded unspeakable deeds, in pictures which survived in Berlin archives and fell into allied hands when Hitler's regime collapsed. But few of those depicting atrocities, or revealing the horrors of the concentration camps, were published during the war years.

While German photography was closely controlled, it was often executed by masters of the art. Goebbels favoured sports photographers for combat work, who had "learned to press the shutter when the ball is on its way to the net". Photo-reporter K. R. Kraupa-Tuskany wrote of his experience on a warship in action: "Photography is a battle for the right moment, a race against time. So I am clinging to the rail of the bridge with my trusty Leica, my camera at the ready, my mouth open, my ears stuffed with cotton-wool because of the noise – breathless!"

Amid Stalin's tyranny, Russian war photographers such as Dmitri Baltermantz worked under much the same restrictions and directives as their German counterparts, but possessed less access to technology. Many so-called combat images of the 1941–45 Red Army are of doubtful provenance. Russian soldiers were almost always depicted in heroic postures. Images of defeat were usually captured and published by the victors, not the vanquished.

If British and American photographers worked under fewer constraints than the Germans, Russians and Japanese, they were likewise subject to censorship. It was made plain that their duty was to serve the Allied cause. Enemy dead were portrayed unsympathetically. A notorious issue of *Life* magazine in August 1945 included a sequence of pictures headed "a Jap burns". They were captioned successively: "1. An Australian soldier on Borneo uses flamethrower on Jap hiding places. 2. Moment later Jap who wouldn't quit ducks out enveloped in flames. 3. With liquid fire eating at his skin Jap skitters through underbrush. 4. Blind and still burning he makes agonizing reach for support, falls. 5. He tries to crawl, falls again. 6. After one last effort the Jap slumps in his own funeral pyre". It was commonplace for Allied photographers to shoot executions of alleged spies or, during the December 1944 Ardennes battle, of German soldiers captured in American uniforms being shot by a firing squad. Allied dead were seldom shown in published pictures. When Robert Capa photographed the body of one of the last American GI's to die in Europe in

---

Opposite **BRITISH TROOPS** *in French trenches in the early part of the war.*
Below **BRITISH TROOPS** *stationed in North Africa, 1942, take time to cool off in the heat.*

1945, the censor obscured the man's face with a balustrade. My own father, a war correspondent for *Picture Post*, told me years later without apology: "What we were doing was part of the war effort".

Life magazine boasted that it showed "war as it really is ... stark, brutal, and devastating". The sheer volume of pictures was astonishing. By December 1944, the censors' office of the Allied Press Bureau in Paris was processing 35,000 photos a week, many taken at mortal risk. Writers such as Ernest Hemingway could sometimes invent stories of their own derring-do. Photographers could never bluster. They had to see for themselves what they recorded. The American David Douglas Duncan arranged for a dive-bomber's wingtank to be modified with a plexiglass nose, so that he could lie prone inside it and shoot images during the plane's attacks. Robert Capa, most famous of all wartime photographers, said: "If a picture's bad, it's because you didn't get close enough". Capa sought to justify his own reputation as an off-duty hell-raiser, writing before D-Day in Normandy: "I know that the war correspondent gets more alcohol, more girls, more money and more freedom than the soldier. He can choose his own place in the stadium when the bloody games start, and he can be a coward without being executed for it. That is his torment. The war correspondent holds his 'stake' in

his own hands, and that stake is his life. He can take it back at the last moment if he wants to. I personally am a gambler. I decided to go in with E Company".

Capa landed among the first American assault troops amid the hell of Omaha beach on June 6, 1944: "it was grey weather for good pictures, but with the grey water and the grey sky the little grey men were very photogenic in front of the surreal design of Hitler's concrete walls". He shot 108 images that day, only to suffer the sort of accident to which every image-maker was vulnerable: all but eight frames were ruined in the darkroom by a careless lab assistant named Larry Burrows – who himself later became a great cameraman, and died in Vietnam.

Many photographers, in World War II as throughout modern history, were young and reckless enough to revel in their experiences. One of them, Robert Silk, said: "If you didn't get killed, [the war] was really a very enjoyable time for a hell of a lot of people including me". But peril was ever present. "The trouble with taking photographs when the air is full of lead", wrote Gene Smith, who was wounded on Okinawa, "is that you have to stand up when anyone with any sense is lying down and trying to disappear right into the earth. I got to my feet... The next thing I remember was a spiral ringing in my ears and I knew... I had been hit".

Many photographers were emotionally scarred by their experiences. The legendary American Lee Miller wrote to *Vogue* describing her experiences in newly liberated France: "I'll try to put it all together for you in some sort of visual piece, because it is harrowing. I, myself, prefer describing the physical damage of destroyed towns and injured people to facing the shattered morale and blasted faith of those who thought 'things are going to be like they were' and of our armies' disillusionment as they question 'is Europe worth saving?'. After taking pictures at

Belsen concentration camp, the British George Rodger said that he would never go to another war. Bert Hardy of *Picture Post* survived the campaign in north-west Europe, and went on to photograph Korea, but was deeply affected by his experiences. Margaret Bourke-White, who took pictures at Buchenwald concentration camp after its liberation, wrote: "Sometimes I have to work with a veil over my mind... I kept telling myself that I would believe the indescribably horrible sights in the courtyard before me only when I had a chance to look at my own photographs. Using the camera was almost a relief; it interposed a slight barrier between myself and the white horror in front of me".

What rendered so many photographs of World War II memorable was that they captured human beings in circumstances of drama, emotion, tragedy, with an immediacy and intimacy hitherto unknown. The machines and tools of war – the planes and ships and tanks – were mere accessories to portrayal of the plight of tens of millions of people. Almost all great war photographs show faces, not places or things. British, American, Russian, German, Japanese photographers alike contributed to creating a vast gallery of images which we are fortunate enough to have inherited. Here are some of the finest, portraying the most terrible struggle in human history in an unforgettable fashion.

Opposite **PARATROOPERS** *of the US 17th Airborne Division on a Churchill tank following their drop near the Rhine, March 1945.*
Below **BATTLE OF THE ATLANTIC.**

PRE-WAR

- RISE OF NAZISM
- SPANISH CIVIL WAR
- JEWISH PERSECUTION
- INVASION OF MANCHURIA
- GERMANY ANNEXES CZECHOSLOVAKIA

GERMANY VOTES FOR THE LAST TIME, *March 1933, before Hitler passed the Enabling Act that effectively made him a dictator. The National Socialist poster on the sandwich board depicts Hitler and President Paul von Hindenburg, and proclaims: "The Reich will never be destroyed if you are united and loyal."*

> " I got my first shoes from Adolf Hitler. All of a sudden my father was given work, the neighbours got work and I was delighted to wear proper shoes for the first time. So of course we all supported Hitler. "

Leo Mattowitz, German soldier who served in Russia

HITLER IN WORLD WAR I is the lowly lance-corporal, on the right, pictured recuperating after being gassed. When news arrived of Germany's surrender, he wrote that he "staggered and stumbled back to my ward and buried my aching head between the blankets and pillow".

HITLER ON THE SWASTIKA-LINED STEPS AT NUREMBERG before his frenzied address to 150,000 of the faithful at the 1934 Nazi rally – scenes immortalized in Leni Riefenstahl's film, *Triumph of the Will.*

EXULTANT REPUBLICAN MILITIA on the Aragon front in the early days of the Spanish Civil War in 1936. Volunteers with high ideals flocked from around the world to join the stand against Fascism, which ended in defeat in April 1939.

FEAR OF AIR-RAIDS STALKS THE STREETS OF BILBAO, May 1937. In April, almost 1,700 people were killed when Guernica was bombed by the German Condor Legion in a terrifying foretaste of the Luftwaffe's Blitzkrieg techniques.

OSKAR DANKER AND HIS GERMAN GIRLFRIEND ADELE are paraded in the streets of Cuxhaven, denounced for their relationship. The girl's sign says, "I am fit for the greatest swine and only get involved with Jews." Danker's reads: "As a Jew, I only take German girls to my room." Section two of the 1935 Laws for the Protection of German Blood and German Honour outlawed extramarital intercourse between Jews and subjects of the German state.

HITLER'S BROWN SHIRTS proclaim their mantras of hate from the doorway of a Woolworth's branch as they enforce a boycott of Jewish businesses in Berlin April 1, 1933.

❝ … it is fair sport for the Nazi children to kick and beat and throw rocks at the little Jews, because that is preliminary training for one of the highest functions of Nazi citizenship and manhood in days to come. ❞

Westbrook Pegler, US journalist, 1936

JAPANESE FRONT LINE IN THE OPENING SALVOES of the invasion of Manchuria, November 1931. In 1937, Tokyo launched a full-scale assault on China, where a million Japanese soldiers fought throughout World War II. The China conflict ended a week after the Japanese officially surrendered to the Allies on September 2, 1945.

AFTER MEETING HITLER IN MUNICH in September 1938, British Prime Minister Neville Chamberlain waves the scrap of paper pledging Germany and Great Britain will never to go to war again and declares, "Peace in our time".

THREE DAYS AFTER CHAMBERLAIN'S PACT WITH HITLER, Nazi troops occupy Czechoslovakia's German-speaking Sudetenland on October 1, 1938, where they are greeted as liberators and heroes.

> " How horrible, fantastic, incredible it is that we should be digging trenches and trying on gas masks here because of a quarrel in a far-away country between people of whom we know nothing! "

Neville Chamberlain, British Prime Minister in radio broadcast, September 1938

A NAZI SALUTE AND FLOODS OF TEARS from one Sudeten woman overcome with enthusiasm for Hitler's legions.

1939

- GERMANY INVADES POLAND
- PHONEY WAR
- EVACUATION OF PARIS AND LONDON
- WINTER WAR

POLISH PRISONERS *march into captivity – their army, with its large force of cavalry, was totally unsuitable for the new warfare. Organised resistance ended in early October, although many Poles fled west to fight with the Allies.*

GERMAN TANKS ROLLED INTO POLAND in the early hours of September 1, 1939. Two days later, on the expiry of an ultimatum demanding their withdrawal, Britain and France declared war on Germany. Italy and Japan asserted their neutrality. Hitler's armies stormed across Poland in what became known as the first blitzkrieg – "lightning war". Polish cavalry and biplanes were no match for Stuka dive-bombers and armoured divisions. Stalin hastened to gather his own share of the spoils, dispatching his forces into eastern Poland, where they met the advancing Germans at Brest-Litovsk on September 19. By the month's end, all Poland was occupied by one tyranny or the other, its government in exile. Wholesale Nazi and Soviet purges of Polish politicians, intellectuals, officers and Jews had begun.

The British and French were unable to offer any practical assistance to their ally. Instead, conscious of their own military weakness, they deployed their armies along the eastern border of France, trained men and fortified positions to wait upon events, and upon Hitler's pleasure. In the air, exploratory British daylight bomber sorties against the German fleet were so brutally savaged by fighters that they were soon abandoned. The government of Neville Chamberlain was unwilling to initiate air attacks on German territory, so the RAF restricted itself to dropping propaganda leaflets, and using its squadrons in France for reconnaissance missions. As a harsh, snowclad winter descended on western Europe, its peoples began to speak of the "Phoney War". They mocked the inertia of the Allied governments and even speculated about whether France and Britain might patch up a deal with Germany.

Only at sea, where the Royal Navy was urged on by First Lord of the Admiralty Winston Churchill, was the conflict prosecuted with energy. British destroyers hunted U-boats, which sank the aircraft-carrier *Courageous* and battleship *Royal Oak* in the first weeks. British heavy units sought out German surface commerce raiders, of which the most notable was the pocket battleship *Graf Spee*. British cruisers brought her to bay off Uruguay on December 15, and fought the fierce action known as the Battle of the River Plate. The damaged *Graf Spee* sought refuge in Montevideo harbour, leaving again two days later only to be dramatically scuttled offshore on Hitler's orders. This was the first notable British success of the war, and British propagandists made the most of it. Of more far-reaching consequences for the war at sea was the British introduction of "degaussing" as a technique for countering deadly German magnetic mines, which had sunk 29 merchant ships since the outbreak of war. This technique effectively reduced the magnetic field of a ship's hull.

The Allies approached the end of the year much vexed about how to prosecute the war. Neither the British nor French possessed any appetite for attacking Germany. When Stalin invaded Finland

" Hitler's armies stormed across Poland in what became known as the first blitzkrieg – 'lightning war'. "

on November 30, It was suggested that the Allies might dispatch ski troops to aid the Finns, but nothing was done. Churchill, as ever, yearned for more aggressive policies. But neither his Cabinet colleagues nor the weak French government shared his belligerence. The British and French people celebrated an uneasy, bewildered Christmas, doubtful about their own national leaderships and unsure of the cause to which they were committed. Rationing of food and petrol, together with a comprehensive "black-out" at night as a precaution against air attack and the mass conscription of young men for military training, were the principal indications that Britain, France and Germany were at war. A long stalemate seemed in prospect on the Western Front.

LEFT *Germany invades Poland, September, 1939*
BELOW *Germans watch as a civilian is forced to shave an Orthodox Jew's beard amid the ruins of a Polish town.*

"It was difficult when all the people around you were being called up. I had a real battle with myself ... But somebody's got to set an example somewhere, even if it means giving up all you've got."

Leonard Gibson, jailed conscientious objector

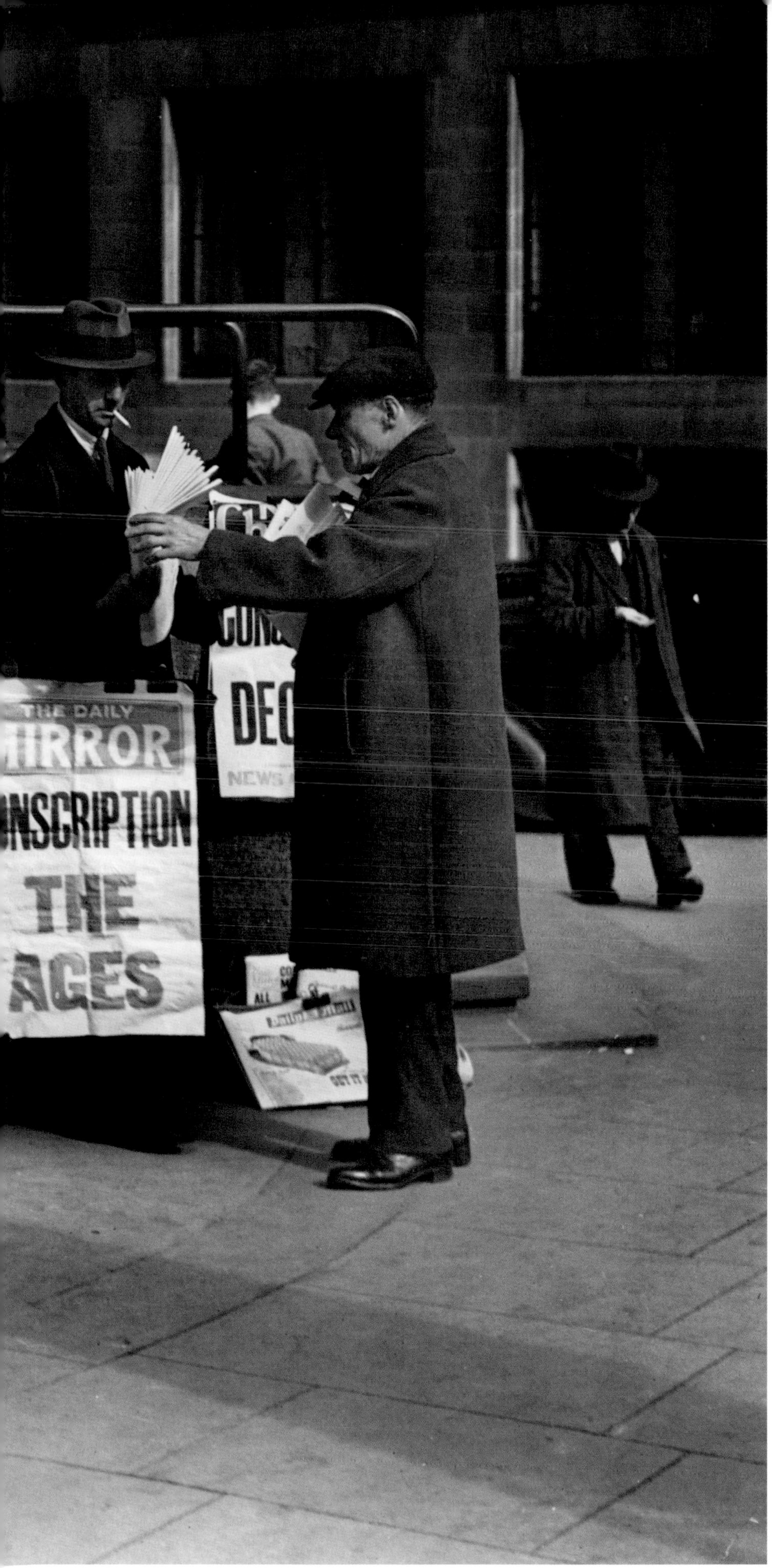

DUTY CALLS FOR FIT YOUNG MEN with the first peace-time conscription in Britain, announced in April 1939. By 1941, single women aged 20 to 30 were being called up while conscientious objectors were branded "pansies" by the popular press.

Right

SCANNING THE SKIES for enemy planes during the opening blitz on Warsaw in early September. In the first mass air attack of the war, Black Monday, September 25, the Luftwaffe bombed their own infantry as well as killing thousands of Poles.

Above

NINETEEN-YEAR-OLD KAROL WOJTYLA (second right), future Pope John Paul II, presents arms at a military training camp in eastern Poland, July 1939. The young Wojtyla worked in a quarry and then a chemical factory under the Nazis while secretly training for the priesthood.

" When the Germans entered my town my grandmother was dying. Her children were gathered around crying and she said that sad times were coming and there would be times when they would envy the dead. "

Joseph Kiersz, Jewish boy growing up in Poland

A GERMAN MOTORISED COLUMN advances up the dusty road into Poland, past a peasant farmer's horse and cart, on the opening day of Hitler's invasion, September 1, 1939.

" The first night there were blackouts all over town ... a young man tried to cross the street and he didn't realise just crossing the street would break the curfew and a German soldier said, 'Halt,' and he kept on running. And he got machine-gunned all the way across.... And because of the way he was machine-gunned, he was completely like cut in half . "

William Luksenburg, *Polish teenager*

WEHRMACHT SOLDIERS SHARE A SMOKE with men of a Soviet tank regiment, in a classic propaganda shot, east of Brest-Litovsk after the partition of Poland. German officers reported to Hitler that the Russians appeared poorly trained and equipped.

WITH EVEN BOY SCOUTS BEING ROUNDED UP AND EXECUTED, these Polish deserters could expect a similar fate, unless spared for slave labour. Almost a million Poles were captured as they fought the German and Soviet invaders alone for five weeks.

ONLY HOURS AFTER BRITAIN DECLARED WAR, these are the first
civilian victims ... survivors from the passenger ship SS *Athenia*, bound
for Montreal from Glasgow and sunk by a U-Boat. The drowning of
118 passengers, 28 of them Americans, highlighted the brutality of the
struggle to which Chamberlain's people were now committed.

“I realised it could not be a troop transport ... the commander
came to the radio room and asked for the Lloyd's Register which
listed all sea vessels... His fingers came to rest on the *Athenia*. He
was, of course, shocked.”

Radio operator Hogel aboard U-boat U-30

BRITISH SOLDIERS QUEUE FOR THEIR JABS in October 1939 – many complained of feeling like pin cushions and suffered painful after effects, but tetanus, typhoid and smallpox could be as lethal as a bullet.

AN INSTRUCTOR EXPLAINS the intricacies of a torpedo to young sailors in October 1939. In some respects the Royal Navy was better prepared for war than Britain's other services, but it was ill-provided with aircraft and anti-aircraft defensive weapons.

"I think we thought it would be like the first war. There'd be the rush forward by the Germans – we'd hold them, then trench warfare..."

Lieutenant-Colonel Alexander Stanier, 1st Battalion Welsh Guards

THERE WAS STILL AN AIR OF FAIRGROUND GAMES

about grenade practice for these recruits during the Phoney War, training in Hampshire before joining the British Expeditionary Force (BEF) in France.

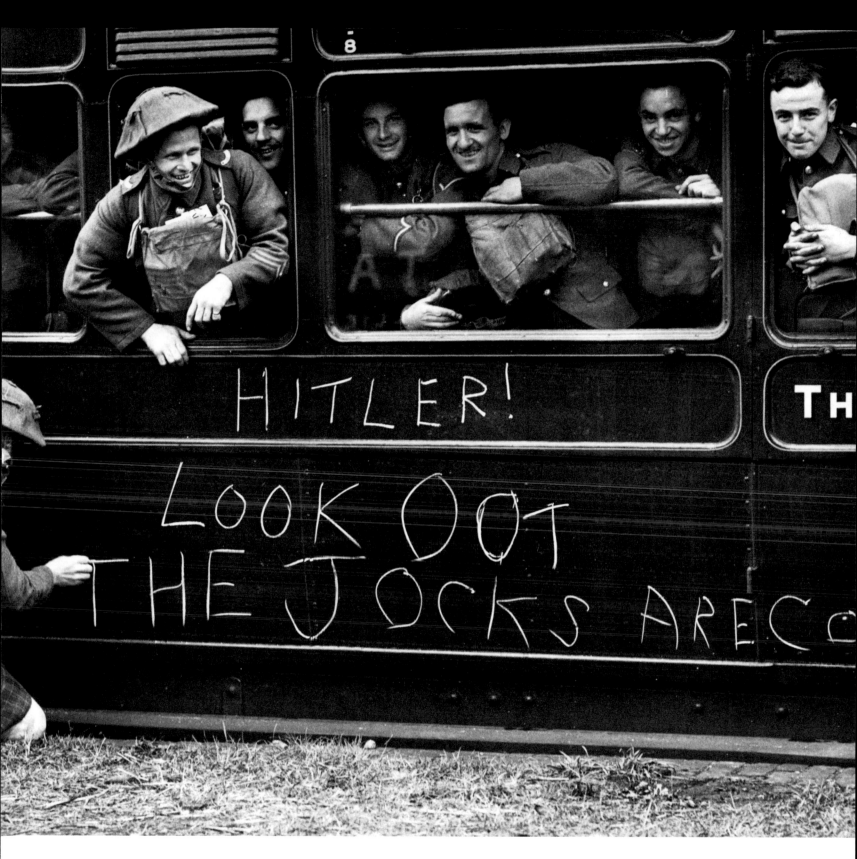

Written on the bus: HITLER! LOOK OOT THE JOCKS ARE C

A SCOTTISH BATTALION OFF TO THE FRONT with a message to strike fear into the enemy. In World War I, Germans mocked the kilted warriors as "Ladies from Hell".

Above

THE FIRST CHILD BORN IN LONDON after war broke out, September 14, 1939, demonstrates a special gas mask on its way home. Filtered air was pumped in by hand bellows. Doom-mongers had advised the government to expect a quarter of a million deaths by poison gas in the first week of the war.

EVACUEES CROWD LIVERPOOL STREET STATION on their way to the safety of East Anglia where many would see cows for the first time. Evacuations began before war was declared. Many children soon returned home, only to be shipped out to the countryside again when the Blitz began.

Previous page

RED ARMY ON THE MARCH. The Nazi-Soviet pact of August 1939 led to the Winter War, with half a million troops invading Finland on November 30. They met strong resistance from a Finnish army outnumbered almost three to one.

SHADES OF 1914–18 as Lieutenant-General Sir John Dill inspects men preparing trenches in France. But these Tommies would at least be spared the lousy, rat-plagued, mole-like experience of the Western Front during a war of swift movement – mostly backwards – when the German juggernaut swept forward in 1940.

MEN OF THE BEF PAY THEIR RESPECTS in a "silent city" of World War I on Armistice Day in France, November 11, 1939. Some cemeteries and monuments were damaged in the 1940 fighting, but most lay undisturbed as the armies of a new generation swept by.

BRITISH SOLDIER HEADING HOME on leave arrives at Euston on December 22, 1939, with the Christmas turkey – this was a propaganda image designed to promote the notion that seasonal supplies were still plentiful.

DECEMBER 1939 AND FRENCH ANTI-AIRCRAFT GUNNERS practise for the expected German onslaught. The French Army possessed 94 divisions and good tanks, but its morale and leadership were poor.

1940

- CHURCHILL APPOINTED PRIME MINISTER
- BATTLE OF THE ATLANTIC
- DUNKIRK EVACUATIONS
- FALL OF FRANCE
- BATTLE OF BRITAIN
- HITLER'S PUSH EAST
- OPERATION COMPASS

TROOPS QUEUE *on the beach at Dunkirk, sometimes for days under German bombing, awaiting evacuation from France at the end of May.*

BRITISH ANTI-AIRCRAFT BATTERY PLAYING FOOTBALL in a snow-covered French field – advance guards of the BEF were in France six days after war broke out. By December, troops strength had reached five divisions.

SCOTS TROOPS ON THEIR WAY TO FRANCE. Thousands ended up as Prisoners of War after the Highland Division was cut off while supporting the Dunkirk evacuation by holding St. Valery. Back home, the authorities appealed in vain for anxious relatives not to tune into German propaganda broadcasts that often named captured servicemen.

BRITISH SOLDIERS FORM A HUMAN CHAIN to load supplies for the fighting in Norway, where the war in the West began in earnest. The Allies took Narvik in late May but were swiftly obliged to evacuate the port. With the campaign plainly doomed, British Prime Minister Neville Chamberlain resigned – and Winston Churchill took charge.

Left

RE-ENFORCEMENTS FOR THE BEF on a troop transport ship to cross the channel to France, to bolster the defences on the Franco - Belgium border.

" We were fighting a losing battle from the time that we arrived in Norway, so morale was not high... you can sustain yourself when you are advancing ... but that's not so easy when you are retreating. "

Captain Desmond Gordon, 1st Battalion Green Howards

SURVIVORS OF HMS *HARDY*, crippled and beached in the first battle of Narvik, are presented to Winston Churchill at Horse Guards Parade in London.

GERMAN TROOPS DASH ALONG a war-torn street of burning buildings in north-east France, late May 1940, where a brave British and French rearguard action bought precious time for the men who escaped from Dunkirk.

BRITISH SEAMEN RESCUED from a flimsy raft following a U-boat attack on a North Atlantic convoy in May 1940. In six years of war the Germans launched more than 1,000 U-boats which sank almost 3,000 ships.

Left

ENGINE ROOM OF A GERMAN PANZERSCHIFF, a hit-and-run commerce raider of the Kriegsmarine. Most of the vessels were swiftly sunk or captured by the Royal Navy.

"We used to sing our English shanties on duty. 'Rolling Home' or 'Blow the Man Down'! Even Adolf Hitler couldn't stop us doing it."

Werner Ritter von Voigtländer, German sailor

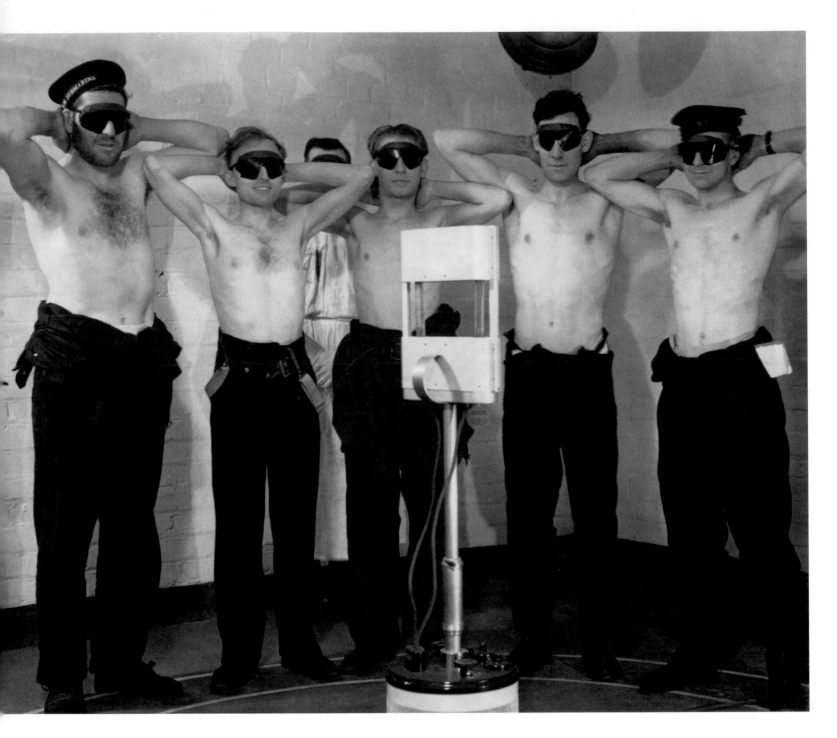

MEN OF THE "SILENT SERVICE", ROYAL NAVY SUBMARINERS, undergoing sun lamp conditioning before venturing beneath the waves. Their exploits may have been put in the shade by their U-boat counterparts, but they played a vital role in helping to clear the seas of enemy ships.

1940 AND HMS *EXETER*, SHIPSHAPE AGAIN AFTER BEING SEVERELY CRIPPLED in the Battle of the River Plate, December 13, 1939, is welcomed back to port.

" The shell which had passed from port to starboard had sliced right through the deck and chopped off the legs of all the telegraphists who were lined up on a bench. "

Able seaman Reginald Fogwill, HMS *Exeter* at the Battle of the River Plate

WARY OF STRAFING FROM ENEMY AIRCRAFT, Royal Ulster Riflemen gather on an improvised jetty of abandoned trucks as they await evacuation during "The miracle of Dunkirk". Thirty Royal Navy ships were lost in an operation originally intended to rescue 45,000 men – in the end, more than 700 craft plucked 338,226 British and French troops from the beaches over nine heroic days.

Right
THE WEARY AND WALKING WOUNDED climb the gangplank of their rescue vessel after arriving back in Blighty from Dunkirk.

A SLIT TRENCH, A BED OF STRAW and a brief "kip" for one of thousands
of men who thought themselves lucky to have reached the French coast alive.

" At Dunkirk … a file of Scottish soldiers came along led by an officer who'd got his arm in a sling. He called out to the bridge, 'What part of France are you taking us to?' One of our officers called back, 'We're taking you back to Dover.' So he said, 'Well, we're not bloody well coming.' "

Ordinary Seaman Stanley Allen aboard HMS *Windsor* at Dunkirk

BRITISH TROOPS GAZE BACK at the scenes of chaos after being rescued from Dunkirk. During the evacuation, six British and three French destroyers were among 200 craft sunk by the Luftwaffe.

SOME OF THE 35,000 FRENCH SOLDIERS CAPTURED while defending
Dunkirk. In the bitter fighting before the evacuation the Germans massacred
some prisoners, most notoriously 97 men of the Royal Norfolk Regiment
machine-gunned at Le Paradis after surrendering to troops of the German
Death's Head Division.

AFTER THE COLLAPSE OF FRANCE, General Charles de Gaulle rallied the remnants of his country's army in London to continue the fight against Hitler. "Frenchies don't pay" was a familiar cry heard on the buses and trams as the capital took the Free French forces to its heart. But many thousands of French evacuees from Dunkirk chose to return to their occupied homeland.

" The Hun got to know that the RAF always sat down to lunch between 12 and one. They seemed to attack at that time. "

Flight Lieutenant Duncan Stuart MacDonald, 213 Squadron, RAF

BATTLE OF BRITAIN HERO Squadron Leader Douglas Bader poses with his Hawker Hurricane Mk.I. Despite having both legs amputated after a 1931 crash, he took command of a wing and shot down several German aircraft before crashing and being taken prisoner in 1941. Bader returned from captivity to lead the victory fly-past over London in June 1945.

"OPS ROOM" AT RAF FIGHTER COMMAND, Bentley Priory, Middlesex. German air raids destroyed a wooden hut and broke a few windows but the underground nerve-centre for the Battle of Britain remained unscathed.

Previous page

"WELL DONE THE RAF," says the original caption with this official picture of pilots resting after an epic aerial battle with "110 Nazi raiders" on July 29, barely three weeks into the Battle of Britain.

BRITISH FIGHTER PILOTS, IN FULL KIT, SCRAMBLE for their waiting planes after radar, observation posts and sector control rooms warn of enemy attack in the Battle of Britain. Many pilots were scarcely out of school – but they were all that stood between the Luftwaffe and Britain's defeat.

RETURNING AIRCREW HITCH A LIFT with a WAAF towing in their plane – as the war progressed, the Women's Auxiliary Air Force took on a widening range of responsibilities for supporting the RAF's squadrons in the air.

AN ARP WARDEN TUCKS CHILDREN INTO THEIR HAMMOCKS as they bed down for the night in the London Underground to gain a respite from the Blitz.

Right

A HOME FROM HOME as Londoners take refuge in Elephant and Castle tube station during the Blitz, November 1940.

❝ When you came back at night on the underground, of the entire platform, only the bit – the 18 inches or maybe two foot – near the edge was left, and all the rest were rows of people with their belongings, cats and dogs and children. ❞

Elizabeth Quayle, London ARP Unit

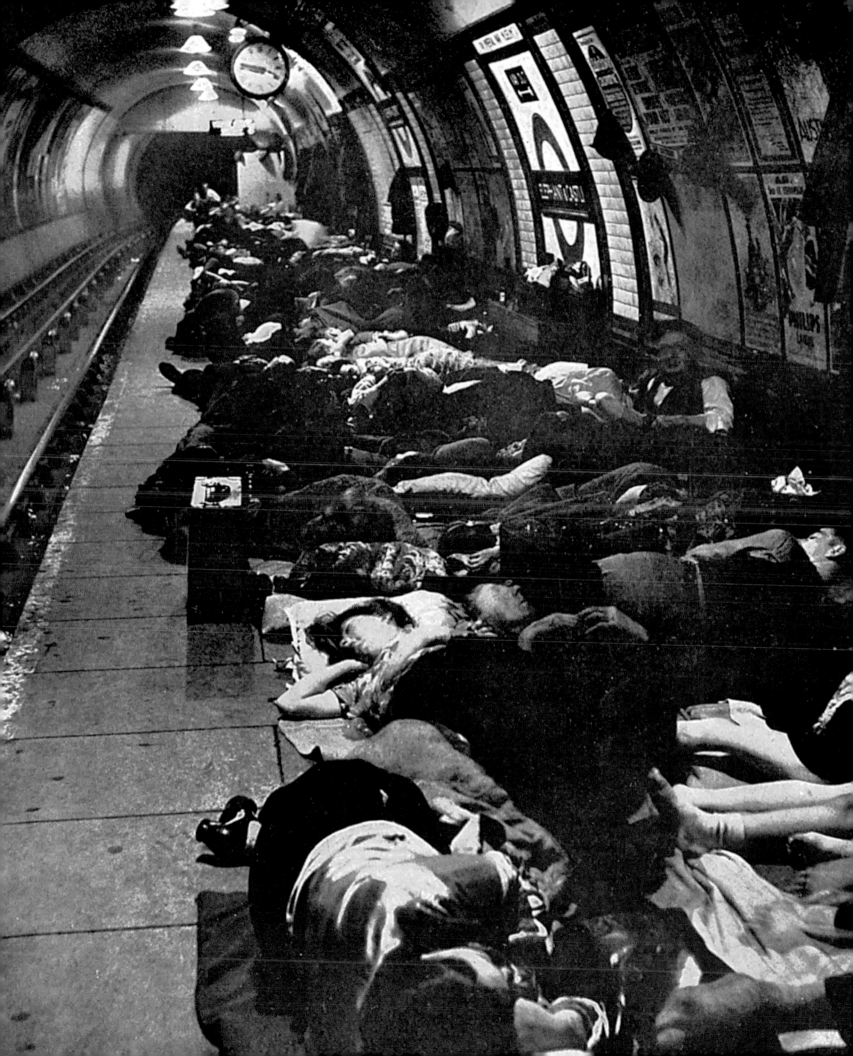

IMAGES OF PARIS UNDER THE NAZI JACKBOOT provided a shocking jolt to US opinion that had resisted peace-time conscription – these were some of the first draft of 21 to 34-year-old Americans called up for training and service under The Selective Service Act of September 1940.

" If Britain should go down, all of us Americans would be living at the point of a gun, a gun loaded with explosive bullets, economic as well as military. "

US President Franklin D Roosevelt

NEW ZEALAND MAORIS PERFORM THEIR TRADITIONAL HAKA war dance on
arrival in England. They would serve with distinction in Greece, Crete and North Africa,
where Second Lieutenant Te Moananui-a-Kiwa Ngarimu was posthumously awarded the
Victoria Cross in March 1943.

SOLDIERS TRAINING IN THE EGYPTIAN DESERT after Italy declared war on
Britain and France in June 1940 and began raiding across the border from Libya. British
forces were heavily outnumbered but more mechanized than the Italians.

AN OFFICER GIVES AN IMPROMPTU BAGPIPE PERFORMANCE during a break from battle in Libya, where the Allies won an overwhelming victory over the Italians in Operation Compass from December 1940 to February 1941. Allied losses were 494 dead and 1,225 wounded while 3,000 Italians were killed and 130,000 captured.

1941

- NORTH AFRICAN CAMPAIGN
- WAR IN THE MEDITERRANEAN
- OPERATION BARBAROSSA
- US SIGNS THE ATLANTIC CHARTER
- JAPAN ATTACKS PEARL HARBOR
- JAPAN'S OFFENSIVES IN THE FAR EAST

SAILORS IN A MOTOR LAUNCH *search the water for survivors from the stricken USS West Virginia at Pearl Harbor after the surprise Japanese air attack of December 7 – what Roosevelt called the "Day of Infamy."*

CHURCHILL MADE A CRITICAL DECISION in March, to risk all Britain's gains in the North African desert in order to dispatch forces to the aid of Greece. Britain's military chiefs allowed themselves reluctantly to be persuaded that the Greek venture might succeed, but the commitment to aid an ally seeking succour was overwhelmingly political, and has remained the focus of controversy ever since. Even as Wavell's forces seized Tobruk and Benghazi in Libya, the first units of Rommel's Afrika Korps began to land at Tripoli, to aid the Italians. The British capture of Abyssinia, together with a naval victory over the Italian fleet off Cape Matapan on March 29, were the last good news to come out of the African and Mediterranean theatres for many months. By early April, Rommel's forces were driving the British eastwards once more. That month, Hitler easily secured Yugoslavia. His armies began to forge southwards into Greece. By April 27, Athens had fallen. British and Australian troops were evacuated to Crete with the loss of all their tanks and heavy equipment. In the Atlantic, British shipping losses to U-boats mounted. Britain's air defences seemed unable to halt the devastation of city after city by the Luftwaffe. Criticism of

Churchill's war leadership became increasingly vocal. On May 20, German paratroops began landing in Crete. A week later, surviving British and Australian troops were taken off by sea, an operation which cost the Royal Navy dearly in ships and lives. The sinking of the battleship Bismarck in the North Atlantic on May 27 provided small consolation for the grievous defeats in Crete and Libya. The morale of the British people, so staunch in 1940, suffered severely under the impact of continuing privation and destruction at home, matched by repeated setbacks to British arms abroad.

The war changed dramatically, however, on June 22. Hitler launched Operation Barbarossa, the invasion of Russia. Three million men attacked on an 1,800 mile front, driving back Stalin's armies in utter disarray, capturing prisoners in the hundreds of thousands, destroying huge numbers of tanks, guns and aircraft. Churchill immediately offered Britain's full support to a new ally, but neither he nor his generals possessed much confidence in Russia's ability to prevail against Hitler's legions. As city after city fell – Minsk, Kiev, Smolensk – and German forces approached Moscow and Leningrad, the legend of Nazi invincibility cast a long shadow over Britain and the world. The British possessed few enough tanks and planes for their own use, but began to dispatch what they could to Stalin. Terrible tales began to seep out of Russia, of wholesale Nazi massacres in the wake of their advance. On August 14, at Placentia Bay off Newfoundland, Churchill met President Franklin Roosevelt aboard the US cruiser *Augusta*. The mere fact of their rendezvous was epoch-making, an earnest show of Roosevelt's support for Britain's cause. The Prime Minister on his return trumpeted the signing of their "Atlantic Charter", with its ringing commitment to freedom. Yet in truth, he was deeply disappointed that the

" The morale of the British people... suffered severely under the impact of continuing privation and destruction at home. "

United States still seemed far from becoming an active belligerent, rather than a mere provider of war material. British bombers were committed to an increasingly heavy assault on Germany. Propaganda trumpeted this enthusiastically, though the RAF was years away from being able to strike effectively at Nazi industry. In the desert, much was made of the Australian defence of Tobruk against Rommel's besieging army. But Wavell's forces were avoiding defeat rather than gaining decisive victories.

In the Mediterranean, the Royal Navy fought a desperate campaign to maintain supplies to the beleaguered and heavily bombed island of Malta. The sinking of the carrier *Ark Royal* by U-boats in November, when *Illustrious* and *Formidable* were already under repair in the US, left the British without naval air support in the Mediterranean. The only important good news for the democracies that November was that Russia survived – and winter had come. Amid snow and ice for which the German armies were wholly unprepared, Stalin's armies fought doggedly on. Russia had lost millions of square miles of territory; whole Soviet armies had vanished; cities were reduced to ruins; tens of millions of people existed in destitution and near-starvation. Yet still Hitler had failed to achieve the victory which he sought. Far-sighted people in the West began to discern a glimmer of hope, that the great Nazi juggernaut had at last met a decisive check.

And then, in the closing weeks of the year, the entire conflict was once again transformed, to become a global war. On December 7, what Roosevelt called "the Day of Infamy", Japanese carrier-borne aircraft struck at the US Navy's principal base at Pearl Harbor. Six battleships were sunk or badly damaged. At the time, this seemed a crippling blow to the power of the United States. Yet posterity perceives it differently. America's aircraft-carriers, together with Pearl's oil storage and repair facilities, survived the attack. They were far more important to the Pacific balance of power

than the old battleships. The assault roused the American people for war as no lesser outrage could have done. When Hitler thereafter declared war on the US, at last Churchill's supreme vision of deliverance was accomplished: the United States with its vast industrial power and prospective military strength was allied with Britain against the Axis. "So we had won after all!", the Prime Minister exulted.

In the weeks which followed, Japan's forces swept across the Philippines and South-East Asia, driving into Malaya and sinking the two great British warships *Prince of Wales* and *Repulse*. Yet shocking as the news was, high as the tide of Japanese victories rose, wise men understood that these reflected the local weakness of the Allies, not the might of Japan. Her economy and industry were weak alongside those of the United States. The year closed amid much bleak news for the Allies from every battle front, with the prospect of more to come. But Churchill was surely right to perceive that, while Allied triumph must be slow to come and the road ahead long and bloody, the final outcome of World War II had become hard to doubt.

LEFT *Improvised bath time for a British Tommy manning coastal defences at Tobruk.*
BELOW *Prisoners of war, Crete, 1941.*

ALMOST 40,000 ITALIAN PRISONERS were rounded up during the attack on Bardia, Libya. Their leader, General Annibale "Electric Whiskers" Bergonzoli, escaped capture only to be seized later at Benghazi.

“The best way of annoying the Bosch is to ask them if they are Italian. They dislike one another intensely.”

Geoffrey Wooler, Royal Army Medical Corps surgeon, North Africa

PILES OF CAPTURED ITALIAN ARMS from the battle at Bardia, Libya, which was taken on January 5, 1941.

"Night after night we set out on patrols, and we'd go so far, then we'd go to ground. Then we just lay there, a listening patrol, lying there for hours. It would get bitterly, bitterly cold, and you just hoped you surprised the Germans and they didn't surprise you."

Private Peter Salmon, 2/28 Battalion, Australian infantry

THE "MOLOTOV COCKTAIL", CHRISTENED in the Winter War in Finland, was used as a last-ditch anti-tank weapon in the Western Desert. This Australian favoured petrol-filled beer bottles, with a grenade attached. British troops preferred milk bottles.

AUSTRALIANS WITH BAYONETS STILL FIXED after capturing three Italian generals in early January during Operation Compass in Libya and Egypt. The "Aussies" forged a legend in the Western Desert as great fighting soldiers, in the tradition of their fathers at Gallipoli.

A FIREMAN CARRIES rescued cage birds through ruins on Clydebank. The Scottish town's vital shipyards survived the air raids of March 13–14, which left just seven houses out of 12,000 undamaged and killed 528 people.

"Amid shouts and frantic gesticulations, we all cowered low as the whistling sound of a bomb was heard near at hand. Then followed a deafening explosion and the crash of falling masonry, and clouds of choking dust and the cries of women and children..."

Unnamed eyewitness quoted in *Clydebank Press*

BULGARIA JOINED THE AXIS to win back territories lost in the Great War and gave a warm welcome to Germany's tanks – including one that claimed to be a personal gift from Hitler to the country's Queen – on March 1.

"THERE WAS A GENUINE SYMPATHY between the German troops and the Bulgarian people everywhere," gushes the caption to this Nazi propaganda photograph of girls in national dress whirling in the arms of Wehrmacht soldiers.

THE ALLIED COMMITMENT TO GREECE ended in defeat and mass evacuation – or captivity in the case of these Australians at Larissa, who were part of a rearguard under constant attack from dive-bombers and pursuing Germans. Some 12,000 Australian and British troops were killed or captured in the abortive campaign, while 50,000 escaped by sea at the end of April.

MEN OF THE RETREATING BRITISH ARMY PASS near Mount Olympus. Despite Allied help, the Greeks were defeated in barely a month and German troops entered Athens on April 27, with the King and the Greek government fleeing to London.

"2 pm – Well, we have just got up off our bellies after a visit from some of the Hun bombers ... we seem to be in a bad spot here. A man will be getting blisters on his belly from diving for cover."

Private Jack Daniel, 2/6 Battalion, AIF

FORMER WORLD HEAVYWEIGHT BOXING CHAMPION Max Schmeling (right) was among the first wave of German troops to parachute into Crete on May 20. In 1945 he visited American PoWs in Germany and handed out autographed photos – "When he left we took the pictures he had given us and did our duty on them in the latrine," said one soldier.

Right
POORLY EQUIPPED AND LACKING AIR COVER, Allied soldiers defending Crete await a German attack in May 1941.

❝We were very much rookie soldiers. I had only actually fired five rounds on the rifle range. As we landed on the quay, a German sniper shot the tallest man in the outfit plumb dead centre in the forehead. This had a very demoralising effect on the men...❞

Edward Hill, Royal Marines on Crete

A GIRL HANDS OUT NEWS SHEETS to Red Army soldiers. The Russian forces included penal battalions made up of 440,000 political and criminal offenders who were given the most dangerous tasks in battle. Few survived.

Left
SOVIET TROOPS MARCHING through Red Square, Moscow, in November in preparation for the counter-offensives which cost countless Russian lives, but stemmed the Nazi tide.

GUERILLA FIGHTERS captured behind German lines on the Eastern Front – "you can't hang all 190 million of us!" was the last cry of one young Russian partisan executed outside Moscow in November.

GERMAN TROOPS AWAIT orders to press on during Barbarossa.
Hesitation was to prove fatal, with Moscow given time to prepare its
defences while Hitler's armies swung south to take Kiev.

INDIAN SOLDIERS SERVING in the desert show off a souvenir of the Libyan fighting – a Nazi flag captured when they overran shallow enemy trenches hacked out of the rocky desert.

Right

SUN-BURNED AND SHOWING THE STAINS if not the strains of the desert war, British troops – one sporting a German greatcoat and cap – perch on a heavy artillery piece at Tobruk, captured in January 1941. The Libyan town was won back by Rommel's Afrika Korps in June 1942, to Churchill's bitter dismay.

❝One sergeant ... was badly wounded and hearing his voice sort of sobbing and calling for his mother seemed so demeaning and humiliating and dreadful ... .❞

Corporal Vernon Scannell, Argyll and Sutherland Highlanders, Western Desert

ADVANCING AUSTRALIAN TROOPS GO TO GROUND as enemy land mines are destroyed in the Libyan desert during Operation Crusader, Auchinleck's big push against Rommel, which achieved some success in December 1941 and the months which followed, before petering out like so many British offensives.

"We were now in the area popularly known as the 'Devil's Cauldron' ... derelict tanks, lorries, guns and dead bodies ... covered in flies, no doubt the same flies that seemed to appear from nowhere to share your bully and biscuits."

Major Gerald Jackson, A Squadron, 6 Royal Tank Regiment

AMID THE WRECKAGE OF BATTLE, a soldier watches enemy bombers attacking Tobruk. In the distance a derelict Italian lorry, loaded with ammunition, has been hit, 12 September 1941.

"Instead of digging graves, the Gurkhas were using the foxholes dug by the Japs. The bodies had rigor mortis, and would not fit, so the Gurkhas were cutting them up and stuffing them into the holes. I stopped this, but they thought I was being pernickety."

Lieutenant Michael Marshall, 4/5 Royal Gurkha Rifles, Arakan

GURKHAS ON JUNGLE MANOEUVRES, October 1941. These were among the best troops of the weak imperial army in Malaya. Later they fought a bloody hand-to-hand rearguard battle with the Japanese, before becoming one of the last units to surrender with the fall of Singapore.

Right
AUSTRALIANS GAIN THEIR FIRST EXPERIENCE of jungle conditions in August 1941 before the Japanese typhoon swept across Malaya and Burma.

JAPANESE PILOTS RECEIVING FINAL ORDERS on board an aircraft carrier before taking off to bomb the US Pacific Fleet at Pearl Harbor, December 7. This is a frame from a Japanese newsreel recording the "glorious victory".

A JAPANESE PILOT KILLED IN THE ATTACK on Pearl Harbor is buried with an American honour guard in the sand dunes where his plane was shot down.

A FIRE-FIGHTING TEAM made up of native Hawaiian women grapple with high-pressure hoses in the aftermath of the attack on Pearl Harbor.

Left

WRECKAGE-STREWN FORD ISLAND NAVAL AIR STATION, Pearl Harbor, with the USS *California* and *Arizona* ablaze on Battleship Row. Tora, Tora, Tora (Tiger, Tiger, Tiger) was the signal transmitted to the Japanese carriers by pilot Commander Mitsuo Fuchida after complete surprise had been achieved. As well as the devastation to Battleship Row, most US planes were destroyed on the ground, but America's own carriers were safe at sea.

" As we reached the boat deck I noted that it was torn up and burned. The bodies of the dead were thick, and badly burned men were heading for the quarterdeck, only to fall apparently dead or badly wounded. "

Marine Corporal E.C. Nightingale, aboard the battleship *Arizona*

1942

- SINGAPORE FALLS TO JAPAN
- TOBRUK FALLS TO GERMANY
- MONTGOMERY APPOINTED: VICTORY AT EL ALAMEIN
- SUBMARINE WARFARE
- GERMANY'S PUSH IN EASTERN EUROPE
- BATTLE OF STALINGRAD

THE FIRST CONTINGENT of the American Expeditionary Force march through a town in Northern Ireland, to start the long wait before going into battle in Europe.

CHURCHILL SPENT THE NEW YEAR in Washington, engaged in strategic planning with President Roosevelt and America's military leadership. "Germany First" was agreed to be the priority. Meanwhile, on the Bataan peninsula west of Manila, and in southern Malaya, US and British forces were relentlessly pressed by the Japanese. By the end of January, the British were confined to Singapore. Churchill demanded that the island should be held to the last, but on February 9 the Japanese crossed the Johore Strait. Less than a week later the British garrison surrendered to an invading force half its size. The Prime Minister was appalled. The experiences of defeat on Crete and at Singapore convinced him that British troops could defeat their enemies only if they had overwhelming superiority. That same sorry week, the battlecruisers *Scharnhorst* and *Gneisenau*, and the cruiser *Prinz Eugen* sailed at high speed from Brest up the Channel to Germany, despite the best efforts of the RAF and Royal Navy to stop them. Their escape – though they were damaged by air-dropped mines – was perceived as a British humiliation in home waters. Churchill's personal standing fell to its lowest level in the war. The Japanese conquest swept on remorselessly, through the Dutch East Indies, the Philippines – where the US garrison was finally forced to surrender in April – and Burma. Japanese carrier-borne aircraft sank the British carrier *Hermes* and bombed Colombo. The "Doolittle raid" on Tokyo by sixteen B-25 bombers achieved a notable propaganda success, but could not erase the shocking list of Allied defeats at Japanese hands. When the Japanese landed in Papua New Guinea, nearby Australia seemed threatened with invasion.

Mercifully, with the coming of summer the picture brightened dramatically. Aided by American code-breakers, who read the enemy's signals, US carrier-born aircraft engaged a Japanese fleet at the Battle of the Coral Sea on May 9. Losses on both sides were about equal, but the US Navy was the strategic victor. A Japanese invasion force was forced to abandon its course towards Port Moresby. The following month, at Midway, a far more decisive success was gained, with the destruction of four Japanese carriers for the loss of one American. Though much bitter fighting lay ahead, the Japanese tide had passed its flood.

In North Africa, by contrast, British fortunes languished. Tobruk fell in June, to an inferior German force. Rommel's army stood inside the frontier of Egypt, threatening the Suez Canal. British prestige plumbed its lowest depths. Churchill, whose own reputation sagged, conducted a purge of Britain's desert commanders. Montgomery assumed command of Eighth Army. It was another decisive moment. Aided by large tank reinforcements and Ultra intercepts of Rommel's signals, the British first repulsed a German thrust at Alam Halfa in August, then in November achieved Britain's only major single-handed land victory of the war, at El Alamein. On November 8, American forces staged the "Torch" landings in French North Africa. Though the Germans sustained the campaign for a further six months, and the year

" The North Atlantic was the focus of Churchill's deapest fears in 1942, with massive losses of merchant ships. "

saw continuing heavy naval losses in the Mediterranean, Allied victory in Africa was assured.

The North Atlantic was the focus of Churchill's deepest fears in 1942, with massive losses of merchant ships to Admiral Doenitz's U-boats. The Royal Navy also paid dearly for sustaining its Arctic convoys to Russia under air and submarine attack. PQ17 in July, which lost 24 of its 36 ships, was the worst, but others suffered grievously. American aircraft progressively joined the RAF's assault on Germany's cities, of which the spring "Thousand Bomber Raids" provided the most dramatic highlights. But the American build-up seemed painfully slow.

The plight of occupied Europe worsened steadily. Hunger and oppression became the daily fare of tens of millions of people. Most ghastly of all was the plight of the Jewish people. Already herded into the ghettoes of Eastern Europe, now they began to be transported to concentration camps to become slave labourers – and in many cases, to face death.

In Russia, German execution squads followed the advancing armies, slaughtering Jews, commissars and alleged partisans wholesale. It was an appalling irony, that Hitler's "Final Solution", the mass murder of Europe's Jews, attained its zenith in the years of Hitler's military eclipse.

The decisive battle of World War II began in August, at Stalingrad. Paulus' Sixth Army reached the banks of the Volga, and laid siege to the city. For the remainder of the winter, the world held its breath as the Red Army fought day by day, yard by yard amid the mountainous rubble, to defend the city. The Germans mounted attack after attack – and were repulsed. For the first time, the western Allies began to dare to hope that Russia might triumph in its titanic confrontation with the Nazi invaders.

LEFT *The Africa Korps range their guns on British tanks in the North African desert.*
BELOW *Italians surrender at bayonet point in the desert war.*

CAPITULATION. BRITAIN, ALREADY STUNNED by the sinking of the *Prince of Wales* and *Repulse* by Japanese torpedo bombers off Malaya, suffered an even greater humiliation with the surender of 138,000 men at Singapore on February 15.

" As a prisoner you have got nothing. You have had a go and you have failed, and you expect to be treated as a normal prisoner of war – but of course, we weren't. "

Sergeant Terry Brooks, Royal Marines

ACCOMPANIED BY A WHITE FLAG, the pathetic figure of Lieutenant-General Arthur E. Percival delivers Singapore to the Japanese – Churchill called it "the worst disaster and largest capitulation in British history".

> *The Times of India carried a colour photo of an RAF plane in North Africa with the shark mouth painted on it. It was an instantaneous hit with our whole group and within days all our planes were adorned with it. It fit the P-40 perfectly.*

Dick Rossi, Flying Tigers' pilot

FLYING TIGERS – men of the 1st American Volunteer Group – examine a souvenir from a destroyed Japanese aircraft. Formed before the US entered the war and disbanded in July 1942, these freelance warriors received double the pay of a USAAF pilot, with a $500 bonus for every Japanese plane they shot down.

GROUND CREW OF AN RAF SPITFIRE SQUADRON in central Burma wrestle with the billowing tarpaulins of their mobile workshop in a premonsoon gale.

RELATIVES SEARCH FOR LOVED ONES among the dead and dying outside Stalingrad.

RED ARMY BATTALION COMMANDER ALEXEI YEREMENKO depicted in an image that became famous around the world. Some 28 million of his countrymen died in the Great Patriotic War. Yeremenko was killed in 1942.

A COSSACK RECONNAISSANCE patrol, serving
with the Germans, reports to an infantry unit
near Ararat, close to the Kuban River, Russia,
December 1, 1942.

MIHAIL SEMKO, one of the famous Don Cossacks who inhabit the region around the Don River in Russia, fought with the Red Army.

"TO HONOUR HER BRAVE PEOPLE I award the George Cross to the Island Fortress of Malta to bear witness to a heroism and devotion that will long be famous in history" – islanders reading King George VI's declaration of April 15, 1942.

Left

CLEARING THE STREETS OF MALTA'S CAPITAL VALLETTA after the Luftwaffe raid of May 11, during 150 days and nights of unrelenting bombing. An offer by German prisoners to rebuild the city's magnificent Royal Opera House after the war was declined.

" It is only a small island, the size of the Isle of Wight, but from its position, anyone could see if we lost Malta in spring of 1942, the effect, not only on the Western Desert, but also on landings in north-west Africa, would be serious. "

Squadron Leader "Laddie" Lucas, 249 Squadron, RAF

Left

PILOT AND CO-PILOT of an RAF Wellington bomber – known as the Wimpy, after Popeye's cartoon pal J. Wellington Wimpy. The Wellington was famously robust and could survive damage that might be fatal to other aircraft.

A RADIO MECHANIC tugs on her "Mae West" (life preserver) before taking off on a test flight at Hatston in the Orkneys, May 26. Only the Russians allowed women to fly in combat but the RAF employed 166 – including the pioneer aviator Amy Johnson who was killed when her plane crashed in the Thames estuary in 1941 – in the Air Trasport Auxiliary, which delivered aircraft to bases.

A BLACK US SOLDIER RECEIVES DIRECTIONS from an English bobby. Discrimination and segregation followed African American servicemen across the Atlantic – in the Cornish town of Launceston there were "blacks only" and "whites only" fish and chip shops.

Right
NAAFI WORKER PAT PARR, of Taunton, Somerset, gives her first US customers a lesson in pounds, shillings and pence.

" The first time that an American soldier comes up to the counter and says 'Hiya Baby!', you will probably think that he is being impudent ... yet to them it will be merely the normal conversational opening just as you might say 'Lovely day, isn't it?' "

NAAFI handbook advice for British shop-keepers

ANTI-AIRCRAFT RANGE FINDERS at action stations on the British carrier HMS *Victorious* during convoy escort duty in April. Even with such protection, two out of three supply ships sailing from the USA to North Russia in 1942 were lost on the outbound or homeward passages.

HMS *MANCHESTER* POM-POM CREW taking a break while escorting the bloody Operation Pedestal convoy, which proved a life-saver for Malta in August. Within days, Italian torpedoes hit the British cruiser and its captain later faced courts martial for scuttling her prematurely.

" The people of Valletta lined the harbour to cheer us, and the military band played 'Hearts of Oak' as we entered... That night we went ashore ... getting gloriously drunk on Ambete, the local wine, but commonly called Stuka juice. "

Able seaman William Cheetham, HMS *Penn*, on the Pedestal convoy

A BLINDFOLDED GERMAN is landed at Newhaven after the disastrous Dieppe raid of August 1942. Survivors brought back a handful of PoWs. The Allies lost 3,600 men, mostly Canadians who were taken prisoner.

Right
COMMANDOS RETURNING FROM DIEPPE with their faces still blacked up. One is wearing a German field cap as a trophy of the raid. Another has lost a leg of his battle-dress trousers.

❝ My feeling is that [Dieppe] was an absolute disaster. It should never have taken place... they had something like 1,000 killed and 2,000 taken prisoner – and what did they achieve? Absolutely nothing. ❞

Major Pat Porteous VC, Royal Artillery

NATIVES OF BECHUANALAND – now Botswana – hauling British army supplies in Lebanon, where their biggest enemy in early 1942 was the bitter cold. Some were later trained as anti-aircraft gunners and used to man smoke generators in the attack on Monte Cassino in Italy. Forty-two were mentioned in despatches.

Right
SOLDIERS SEARCHING FOR FRESH WATER in North Africa peer down a deep well – both sides were known to pollute precious supplies with salt to deny them to the enemy.

Below and right

THE TWO TOWERING FIGURES of the see-saw battles in North Africa. Rommel's Afrika Korps broke into Egypt (right) but was denied decisive victory by inadequate strength, loss of air superiority and over-extended supply lines. Montgomery (below) built up his air and ground forces until he struck the decisive blow at El Alamein in October, while Rommel lay on a sickbed back in Germany. Hitler's most famous general took his own life by poisoning rather than hang for his part in the July 1944 assassination plot against the Fuhrer.

" Montgomery came up in a tank... He was wearing this Australian hat, with all the badges that were around the brim, and a pair of 'Bombay bloomers' ... much wider than normal. Now, dressed in that hat and shorts, and with his thin legs, he looked like matchsticks in a pair of boots. Very high-pitched voice – and he didn't look like a general at all. *"*

Sergeant James Fraser, Royal Tank Regiment

> "In these desert conditions one's shirts got dark with sweat each day. There was no hope of washing them; water was much too precious. The shirts got darker and encrusted with dust and eventually disintegrated."

Signaller James Bostock, Durham Light Infantry

TWO MEN SAW THE OPENING OF THE ALLIED OFFENSIVE in the Western Desert from the enemy lines. They were members of a Wellington crew trudging back across the desert from El Adem where their aircraft had been forced down. They walked for over three weeks.

A BRITISH BOFORS GUN passes a dead German soldier in the desert while pursuing the retreating enemy after El Alamein in early November.

❝ After years of being pushed about by the Axis forces, at last we were holding our own and doing a bit better than holding our own. We were actually beating them. Everybody could see we were beating them. ❞

Corporal Peter Taylor, 2nd Battalion, Rifle Brigade

LOG LIFTING was one way of keeping the men fit and occupied away from the front line when the heat was off in the desert campaign.

MONTY'S FORCES IN THE WESTERN DESERT, here practicing P.T., numbered about 230,000 men and 1400 tanks whereas the Afrika Korps and its Italian allies mustered only 80,000 men and 500 tanks by October 1942.

" Our supplies were cut off absolutely. Ammunition, fuel for our vehicles and bread soon came to be worth their weight in gold. "

General Eric Hoepner, commander of Panzer Group 4 on the invasion of Russia

SOLDIERS OF THE GERMAN engineering corps cross a river swollen by the first autumn rains on the central front in Russia.

HEAVY PLANT from the bombed out Red October steel plant in Stalingrad provides cover for Soviet soldiers who were ordered to "hug" the enemy – get close enough for hand-to-hand combat so the Germans could not call in air strikes without killing their own troops.

> " We used to saw the legs off frozen Russian corpses in order to get their warm felt boots. We stood them up against a stove and when the legs had thawed, we pulled them out and dried off the boots. "

Edmund Bonhoff, German soldier on the Eastern Front

A MACHINE-GUNNER keeps watch as his Red Army comrades eat their meagre rations in the Stalingrad "meat grinder". By November, the Russians had turned the tables and were launching counter-attacks.

CONTRARY TO POPULAR images, only a few Allied shells carried personal messages for Adolf Hitler. It was thought to be good for morale at home that civilians should see men, like this desert mortar crew, repaying Germans for the Blitz.

TURKEYS FOR THE BOYS in the Middle East. In truth, however, the nearest most Eighth Army soldiers came to seasonal fare in December 1942 was to share a bottle of beer between four.

1943

- GERMAN DEFEAT AT STALINGRAD
- GERMAN SURRENDER IN NORTH AFRICA
- BATTLE OF KURSK
- OPERATION POINTBLANK
- SICILY LANDINGS
- US ISLAND-HOPPING CAMPAIGN
- NEW GUINEA AND THE SOLOMONS

GERMAN PARATROOPERS ON GRAN SASSO *after successfully carrying out Hitler's orders to free deposed dictator Mussolini — held captive in a mountain hotel, September 1943.*

SOVIET SOLDIER FIRING FROM THE BATHTUB of a ruined house in Stalingrad in January 1943. A city of 850,000 people was reduced to just 1,500 souls by the end of the fighting, almost all surviving civilians having been evacuated.

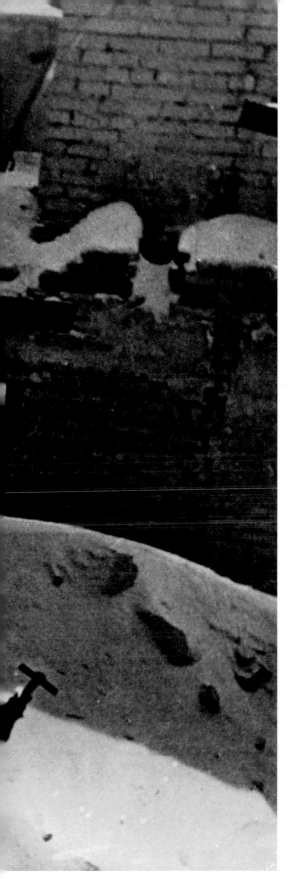

A GERMAN SOLDIER of the Sixth Army, trapped in a dug-out in Stalingrad as the Soviet Red Army advance to recapture the city, January 1943.

"RED ARMY SOLDIERS CLOSE IN ON THE ENEMY," says the official caption to this staged grenade attack. Of the 91,000 Germans who surrendered after Stalingrad, barely 5,000 would live to see their homes again. German troops ended the battle without ammunition, food or effective command.

HAGGARD, SHAMBLING RUSSIAN SOLDIER – but at Stalingrad he and his comrades had shattered the myth of Nazi invincibility.

AMID THE SMOKING RUINS of the Warsaw Ghetto, civilians are herded together at gunpoint during the Jewish revolt against mass deportation to Nazi death camps. The rebellion lasted from April 19 to May 16, to be followed in 1944 by a nationalist uprising that claimed an estimated quarter of a million Polish lives and destroyed what was left of Warsaw.

" The Germans were going from house to house ordering people to come down or they would blitz the houses, and the people were jumping from the houses, killing themselves. My wife, who had escaped outside by then, saw with her own eyes Jews jumping from windows. She heard Poles standing nearby laughing and saying, 'The Jews are being fried.' "

Martin Parker, Polish Jew in the Warsaw ghetto

JEWISH FIGHTERS EMERGE from a blazing house with hands raised after SS-Gruppenführer Jürgen Stroop, SS chief in Warsaw, ordered the ghetto to be burned down and anyone left to be immediately killed or dispatched to death camps. The image is from Stroop's personal photo album. He was found guilty of war crimes and executed – in Warsaw – in March 1952.

ALLIED SPECIAL FORCES – the legendary Chindits – aboard an evacuation plane following Operation Longcloth, in which 3,000 men marched over 1,000 miles through the jungles of north Burma, deep behind enemy lines.

GURKHA SOLDIER CARRYING A WOUNDED COMRADE to the rear during the
Arakan campaign. In one assault, the Japanese massacred the entire British and Indian
medical team at a field hospital and bayoneted the wounded in their beds.

A WELCOME BREW-UP for 8th Army signallers as the desert campaign swept from Libya into Tunisia. Note the "jerry can" which the British adopted from a German design.

Right

THE LONG RANGE DESERT GROUP (which also guided the SAS on its raids) were heavily armed and laden with water and fuel for weeks of operations behind enemy lines in the desert war. In October 1942 Hitler ordered all captured Commandos "to be slaughtered to the last man", though in North Africa German troops seldom killed prisoners.

" I always had on board guys who argued. They weren't really controllable, but harnessable. "

Colonel David Stirling, commanding the 1st SAS Regiment

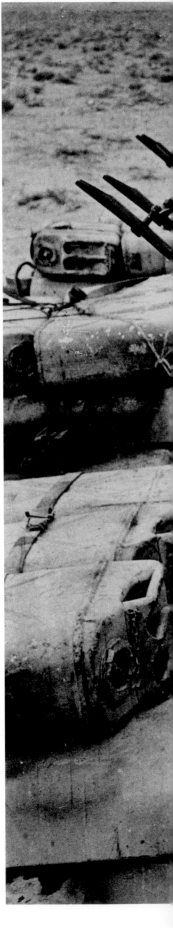

WOUNDED TOMMY AND ENEMY PRISONER, with matching slings, light up after fighting in Tunisia, March 1943. After Montgomery's victory at El Alamein, the Germans regrouped with Italian forces in Tunisia and held out until their final surrender in North Africa on May 13.

Above

US FORCES under Major General George S. Patton roll into the Tunisian stronghold of Maknassy without a fight and with a welcoming handshake from locals on March 22. Patton was determined his men should look, as well as fight, like the best soldiers in the world – he tried to make them wear neckties.

❝ Two things won the psychological war in my view – a cup of char and a fag. Whatever morale a Tommy was in beforehand, it's right high up after he's had his fag and a cup of char. ❞

Sergeant John Longstaff, 2nd Battalion, Rifle Brigade, North African campaign

P-47 THUNDERBOLT CREWS being briefed before a mission. A tough plane to fly, the Thunderbolt cost the lives of 18 test pilots during development in America. USAAF Major Don Blakeslee recorded the aircraft's first "kill" on April 15, 1943.

TWENTY-FIVE-YEAR-OLD WING COMMANDER GUY GIBSON and his crew board their Avro Lancaster, May 16 – christened Admiral Prune II – for the Dambusters raid, which smashed two Ruhr dams with Barnes Wallis' bouncing bombs. Gibson was awarded the Victoria Cross. He was killed returning from another bombing mission in September 1944.

THE RED ARMY ATTACKING across open country in broad daylight – Soviet recklessness with lives contributed to losses at Kursk in July of 250,000 killed and 600,000 wounded. Operation Zitadelle was intended by Hitler to reverse defeat at Stalingrad, but the Germans were repulsed in one of the decisive battles of the Eastern Front.

SOVIET T34S ARE FLAGGED towards the greatest tank engagement of the war at Kursk. The Germans rushed their latest armour forward to face the Russian threat, but most of the new Panther tanks broke down on the first day, and heavyweight Elefant tanks proved sitting ducks for Molotov cocktail attacks.

HEAVILY-LADEN BRITISH TROOPS landing in Sicily, July 1943. The initial assault was marred by heavy casualties among paratroops, many of whose planes were fired on by reckless ships' gun crews.

❝ The American invading force was brought from Africa to Sicily in three immense fleets sailing separately. Each of the three was in turn broken down into smaller fleets. It was utterly impossible to sail them all as one fleet. That would have been like trying to herd all the sheep in the world with one dog. ❞

Ernie Pyle, US war correspondent

BAREFOOT SICILIAN PEASANT FAMILY watch as US combat medic Harvey White gives blood plasma to a young GI badly wounded as the Germans were being driven from the toe of Italy, August 9.

" They were the half-crazed, grief-shocked people who welcomed the Fifth. Hysterical at deliverance from the Nazis, they bombarded the Allied soldiers with flowers, fruits, vivas and kisses. Men and boys came out of holes, too, carrying rifles and grenades... Some... were murderers and thieves whom the Germans, with diabolic humour, had released from Naples' jails. "

Time magazine report from Naples, October 11, 1943.

A SICILIAN GIRL feeds grapes to a conquering hero of the British 8th Army after four days of fierce fighting around Catania in August. Most Italians welcomed the invaders, and Italian troops surrendered readily.

Right
AMERICANS ARRIVE in the mountain town of Pollina after the invasion of Sicily, the largest amphibious landing in history until D-Day. The Allied advance failed to prevent 40,000 Germans, 62,000 Italians and vital equipment from escaping across the straits of Messina to fight another day.

❝ They had all sorts of things booby-trapped. ... guy would say, 'Oh, a souvenir,' and boom! You can't convince the American soldier that he shouldn't look for souvenirs... he has to lose his arm before he realises... ❞

Major Roy Murray, 4th battalion, US Rangers in Italy

A TRUCK CARRYING US TROOPS through a rubble-filled street in Naples, captured by the Fifth Army on October 1. Six days later, 100 soldiers and civilians were killed by a huge German delayed-action charge, which blew up the city's post office.

A KITCHEN SHOWING SCARS of house-to-house fighting provides a vantage point for a British 8th Army soldier, armed with a US Thompson, after the fall of Naples in October. Before the war the British Army rejected sub-machine guns, claiming that they encouraged soldiers to waste ammunition.

BRITISH SPECIAL FORCES SOLDIER uses his backpack as shade from the sun as he returns to India after surviving a deep penetration mission in Burma.

IRREGULAR FORCES recruited from the hill tribes of north Burma were armed and trained by the British to harass the Japanese behind their own lines.

Above and right

US TROOPS ON TARAWA ATOLL in the Pacific, November 20, where few
kept smiling for long. Wading ashore on razor-sharp coral, many men were
mown down before reaching the beach. Tanks and artillery made it ashore on
the second morning. Two days later the Marines had won their bitter fight
and found themselves sampling captured Japanese beer and sake. Of the
4,700 Japanese on Tarawa just 17 were left alive.

1944

- CASSINO AND ANZIO

- ROME FALLS TO THE ALLIES

- OPERATION OVERLORD

- OPERATION MARKET GARDEN

- THE WARSAW RISING

- THE BATTLE OF THE BULGE

- ALLIED GAINS IN BURMA AND THE FAR-EAST

THE VAST INVASION ARMY *streams ashore following the June 6, D-Day landings.*

"When we landed at the Anzio beachhead, we didn't go in for three or four days, then, when we made the push, Jerry had brought up reinforcements and we didn't get very far. If we'd gone straight for Rome, we could have captured it in the first two days."

Corporal James Orr, Irish Guards

AMERICAN TROOPSHIPS AT ANZIO, 30 miles south of Rome, where the Germans were taken completely by surprise in January 1944 – in under 24 hours 36,000 men and 3,200 vehicles were ashore with total casualties of just 13 killed, 97 wounded and 44 missing. After that, however, a nightmare slogging match began.

THE ALMOST BLOODLESS LANDING at Anzio turned into a vicious battle of attrition with the Allies confined in their beachhead until late May. These men of the Cheshire Regiment were taking cover in a captured German trench on the eve of the breakout of May 23–24.

PILOTS OF THE ALL-BLACK 332nd Fighter Group, the famous Tuskagee Airmen or "Redtails" – named after their training base in Alabama – serving in Italy. They claimed to be the only US fighter outfit of the war never to lose a bomber while on escort duties.

11PM, THE NIGHT BEFORE D-DAY – commanders of 22nd Independent Company pathfinder unit synchronise watches before taking off from Oxfordshire to parachute behind enemy lines and mark out landing zones for the airborne invasion of Normandy.

MEN OF 4 COMMANDO being briefed on their D-Day role by Lieutenant-Colonel R. W. P. Dawson – they were among the first British troops to hit the Normandy beaches on June 6 and Lieutenant-Colonel Dawson became an early casualty.

Above

PARIS, HERE WE COME – these Royal Engineers on the Channel passage were promised a fine welcome in France by this Forces' guidebook. But first there was a bitter battle to be won.

AN AMERICAN GI hugs the sand amid swirling waters and German beach
attacks in the Easy Red sector of "Bloody Omaha" beach – Robert Capa's classic,
raw image vividly captures one of the most terrifying moments of D-Day.

" The men from my barge waded in the water... The boatswain, who was in an understandable hurry to get the hell out of there, mistook my picture-taking attitude for explicable hesitation, and helped me make up my mind with a well-aimed kick in the rear. The water was cold, and the beach still more than a hundred yards away. The bullets tore holes in the water around me, and I made for the nearest steel obstacle. "

Robert Capa, photographer

MEN OF US 1ST DIVISION, "The Big Red One", wade ashore on the morning of June 6. Those who survived the hail of machine-gun bullets had to storm heavily-wired coastal bluffs studded with enemy pillboxes.

❝ ... The senior army officer gave us a briefing ... 'Don't worry if all the first wave of you are killed,' he said, 'We shall simply pass over your bodies...' What a confident thought to go to bed on. *❞*

Able Seaman Ken Oakley, Royal Naval Commando

A NEWSREEL FRAME showing Royal Navy commandos approaching Sword Beach on June 6.

Right

BRITISH TROOPS OF THE FIRST ASSAULT WAVE landing amid haze and smoke on Sword Beach. Casualties litter the shoreline and men struggle to recover dead and wounded comrades before a new wave of landing craft overruns them.

MEDICS TENDING wounded US infantry in the shelter of a sea wall at Utah beach, furthest west of the five D-Day landing zones, where casualties were light compared to the carnage at Omaha.

Right

THE LONGEST DAY is over for two desperately burned British casualties – almost certainly tank crew – photographed by the gangplank of their hospital ship.

" When we came in ... it was just a hell of a mess ... explosions, guys lying dead on the beach, guys getting killed right there on the ramp. I had to roll them off. I didn't know if they were alive or dead. "

Jack Hoffler, US Navy gunner at Omaha Beach

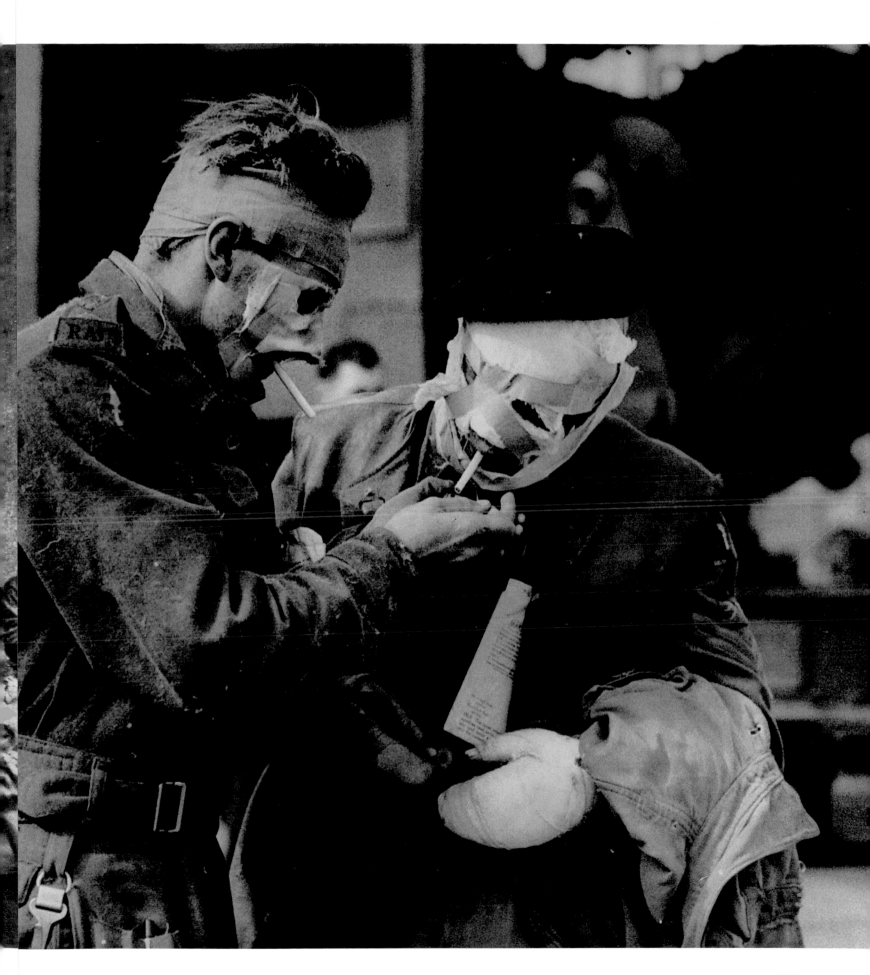

AFTER TWO MONTHS OF BITTER FIGHTING IN NORMANDY, the Allied
breakthrough came. As Montgomery's and Patton's forces raced to encircle German
troops in the Falaise pocket, Royal Engineers lay a Bailey bridge across the river Orne.

Right
BRITISH TROOPS PAUSE in Nijmegen during Operation Market-Garden – the
September 1944 dash for the Rhine bridge at Arnhem. Dogged German resistance on the
single road north into Holland made this "a bridge too far".

SOLDIERS OF THE BRITISH 1st Airborne division before emplaning in C-47 Dakotas for the drop on Arnhem. The codename for the airborne operation to seize a bridgehead on the Rhine was "Market" and for the ground advance "Garden".

MEN OF THE WAFFEN SS, alleged snipers, taken prisoner in the suburbs of Arnhem – the youngest is 17 years old. Their British captors stand behind them.

" These snipers were the very devil and picked off more of our men than I care to think about. "

Neil Walker, Army Film and Photographic Unit, Arnhem

A NEW TERROR FOR CIVILIANS who had stoically endured the Blitz in 1940 ... a dazed and bloodied survivor is dug out alive after a V-1 "doodlebug" attack on London. Rescuers pass the victim a cloth to wipe her face.

Right
FIREMAN AND CIVILIAN HELPERS carry children from shattered homes and shelters in London following a "doodlebug" attack. The V-1 flying bombs killed 6,000 people between June 1944 and March 1945.

" The doodlebugs were pretty frightening, but the V-2s were terrifying. Perhaps we were tired by that point in the war, but we were much more scared than when the bombs were raining down on us during the Blitz. "

Myrtle Solomon, civilian in London

" After Normandy, in early August 1944, our position came under fire. We were surrounded, they were shooting from every direction, and almost everyone in my unit died. It was awful "

Private Fritz Jeltsch, 214 Regiment of the German Army

GERMANS CAPTURED by US forces at Cherbourg following the Allied invasion of Normandy.

US MILITARY POLICE search German SS prisoners swept up in the Allied advance through France, July 31, 1944.

"French police could hardly control the cheering crowds. Every citizen of Paris must have been there! French girls were breaking into our ranks to hug and kiss our soldiers. Despite all this, we did maintain order."

Colonel Charles Crain, US Army, in Paris for the liberation

A HOLLYWOOD GLAMOUR SHOT of a US army lieutenant alongside a French resistance fighter. The nonchalant gendarmes in the background suggest that they are not in great peril.

Right

THE LIBERATION OF PARIS, August 25 – police, American soldiers and resistance fighters escort German prisoners through jubilant crowds in front of the Opera.

FIRST WAVE OF MARINES hit the beach in the US amphibious attack on Saipan, June 15. Two men are already down. Bitter Japanese resistance ended with a suicidal "Banzai" attack in July. Hundreds of civilians hurled themselves to their deaths from sea cliffs rather than surrender.

We protected ourselves as best we could, covering ourselves with mattresses. When the air battle ended at dusk, as it did daily, we went outside. The spectacle was awe-inspiring ... the surrounding mountains aflame, covered by a dense black smoke."

Sister Maria Angelica Salaberria, missionary on Saipan

A BEWILDERED CHAMORRO NATIVE of Saipan and his wounded child were among thousands caught between Japanese and American fire in the battle for control of the island, July 1.

GERMAN TROOPS PASS ABANDONED and burning US vehicle at the start of the Ardennes Offensive in December. This was Hitler's last desperate throw of the dice in the West, aimed at recapturing Antwerp.

SCENE FROM CAPTURED GERMAN PROPAGANDA film showing an
SS Panzergrenadier during the desperate assault in the West, which shocked
the Allies and became "the battle of the Bulge".

BRITISH ARMY MOTORCYCLIST signals a troop convoy past a makeshift German grave as the Allies pressed on east towards the German border after the fall of Paris.

A 15-YEAR-OLD LUFTWAFFE conscript sobs with fear and humiliation after being captured when his anti-aircraft position was overrun on December 31, during the American counter-attack in the Ardennes.

1945

- IWO-JIMA
- OKINAWA
- BATTLE OF BERLIN
- GERMANY SURRENDERS
- HIROSHIMA AND NAGASAKI
- JAPAN SURRENDERS

PRIVATE MIKHAIL MININ *risked bullets and bombs to plant the Soviet flag on the Reichstag, securing it with his trouser belt. But no camera captured the emblematic moment so it was re-enacted – without Private Minin – two days later in comparative safety.*

" At dawn the vultures arrived to clean up what the crocodiles had left... Of about 1,000 Japanese soldiers that entered the swamps of Ramree, only about 20 were found alive. "

Bruce Wright, British naturalist attached to the Royal Marines

A SHERMAN TANK ENCOUNTERS a newly liberated elephant after the capture of Meiktila, March 29, 1945, a major victory of the campaign in Burma, the longest fought by the British army in World War II.

Left

IMPROVISED ALFRESCO DINING for British soldiers beside a Buddhist temple during the campaign to expel the Japanese from Ramree Island, off Burma. Many of the retreating enemy met their fates in the crocodile-ridden, scorpion-infested swamplands of the interior.

SURVIVORS OF BUCHENWALD "extermination factory". Although originally designed for political prisoners, Jews were shipped there by the Nazis to die in their thousands – starved or murdered – when camps in the East were overrun.

Opposite
SURVIVORS OF AUSCHWITZ-BIRKENAU, liberated by the Red Army in January 1945. In the rush to greet their rescuers some inmates died on electric fences that surrounded the camp where more than a million victims perished.

❝ ... a German soldier attempted to surrender to the Americans, but was intercepted by a prisoner with a four-foot wood log. He just stood there and beat him to death – of course, we didn't bother him. ❞

Corporal Fred Mercer, 69th Signal Battalion, 20th Corps, 3rd Army

A LIBERATED CONCENTRATION CAMP INMATE turns accuser. The camp guards at Dachau, notorious sadists, had often hurled prisoners' caps into the forbidden zone beside the wire. Victims were shot if they attempted to recover them, bludgeoned to death if they failed to do so. Now, the hour of retribution had come.

❝ Control was gone after the sights we saw... one of the soldiers gave one of the inmates a bayonet and watched him behead the man... A lot of the guards were shot in the legs so they couldn't move... ❞

Jack Hallet, US Army liberating Dachau

A GERMAN WOMAN CHOKES as she is forced to walk among the corpses of concentration camp victims killed while being transported from Buchenwald to Dachau. Some German guards were summarily executed by US troops along with their dogs.

HAUNTED FACES OF DEFEATED Germans, mostly Volkssturm home guards hastily conscripted for the defence of Hitler's capital as the Red Army launched the Vistula-Oder operation, February 1945.

Right
A LINE OF 1,000lb bombs provides a footbridge across a flooded RAF dump after heavy rain and snowfall in eastern Italy, February 1945. The Allies – including Polish, Indian, Italian and Brazilian troops, and US 'Buffalo Soldiers' – renewed the offensive in the spring and the last of the Axis forces in Italy surrendered on April 29.

REICH MINISTER Joseph Goebbels celebrated a last futile victory when he visited the town of Lauban, Lower Silesia, on March 9, after its brief recapture from the Russians.

Right

BERLIN, APRIL 1945: a teenager shares a foxhole with a veteran, waiting with a Panzerfaust to meet the Red Army after Hitler ordered the mobilization of every able-bodied male for the final stand.

" Among the Fritzes we took captive was a 59-year-old German and he didn't have a tooth in his head but this bastard was fighting like some brainless automaton. "

Red Army officer

TWO BRITISH SIGNALLERS admire the work of a prankster who has put his own slant on Allied victory by spelling out 'Heil Stalin and Churchill and Truman' at Berlin's Olympic Stadium. The score reads 'Arsenal 19, Chelsea 0, Heinz 57'.

"" We women proceeded to make ourselves look as unattractive as possible to the Soviets by smearing our faces with coal dust and covering our heads with old rags, our make-up for the Ivan. ""

Dorothea von Schwanenfluegel civilian in Berlin

BERLINERS emerge from their cellars and hideaways into the devastated streets of their city after Hitler's suicide and the capitulation of Germany.

Above and right

US SOLDIERS ON OKINAWA, bloodiest land battle of the
Pacific war. Many thousands of civilians died in the struggle, or
killed themselves rather than surrender to the Americans.

" ... the inhabitants ... have been forced into military
service and hard labour while sacrificing everything they
own as well as the lives of their loved ones. ... I feel deeply
depressed and lament a loss of words for them. "

Rear Admiral Minoru Ota, Japanese Navy, Okinawa

IN MARCH, 1945, the Japanese were driven from Mandalay and by
April 14 the "Race for Rangoon" had reached Yamethin where these
British soldiers scoured the ruins of the railway station on the Main
Central Burma Railway for suicide bombers.

" A man with a blood-covered bandage round his leg had a better chance of being excused work than a man dying of dysentery or malaria. The Japanese would kick the wound to see if he screamed before excusing him... "

Lieutenant James Bradley, Royal Engineers, Japanese PoW

FREED PRISONERS OF WAR in Rangoon. The soldier second right is Corporal Usher whose life was saved by a major of the Indian medical service who amputated his leg without anaesthetic after infection set in.

VICTIMS OF THE FIRST US ATOMIC BOMB, dropped on Hiroshima on August 6. Scientists on the "Manhattan Project", including some who had fled Nazi Germany and Fascist Italy, developed the device that killed at least 70,000 people.

Below

TWENTY-FOUR HOURS after the second atomic bomb was detonated above Nagasaki on August 9, a mother and child clutch rice balls, emergency rations provided by student relief teams.

A MAN PAINTS a boundary sign on a street in Berlin in 1948, demarcating the British Sector of the city following the partition of Berlin.

Left

WASHDAY IN THE WASTELAND that is Berlin after the Red Army and Allied bombers had reduced the city to ruins. Women gather at a water hydrant beside a wrecked scout car. Hundreds of thousands of Berliners were homeless and starving.

❝ What was Berlin like at the end? Ruined, destroyed, incinerated. The civilians were in cellars, scared ... they left the cellars only to fetch water and maintain a minimum of hygiene. ❞

Ulf Ollech, teenager in Berlin

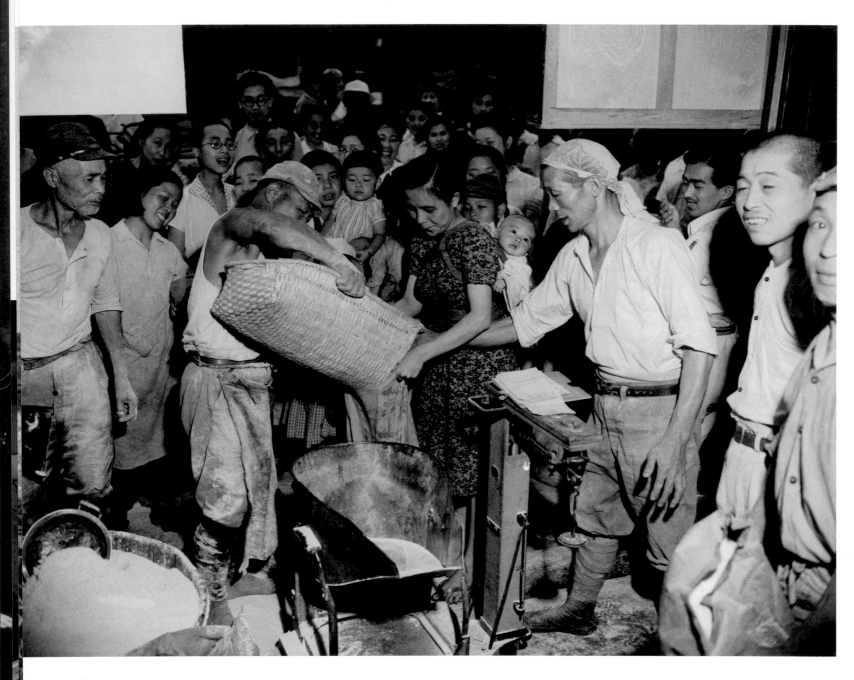

COMING TO TERMS WITH DEFEAT and a Japanese emperor ready to renounce claims to being a god, the starving people of Japan were astonished by the generosity of their conquerors. Here, in Tokyo, they queue to collect a daily ration of 297 grams of wheat flour and rice provided by America.

HOUSEWIVES COMPARE FISH RATIONS at a time of chronic food shortages which persisted for years after the war. In the early days of peace, bananas reappeared in Britain – a child in Yorkshire died after consuming four of them – but staples like eggs and butter remained rationed and the wheat content of bread was reduced to 1942 levels.

Royal Naval commandos 212
Royal Oak, HMS 24
Royal Ulster Rifles 60
rum ration 180
Russia, invasion of 86

S
Saipan 230-1
Salerno, Battle of 164
Scharnhorst 124, 165
Schmelling, Max 100
Scottish troops 36-7
  Highland Division 51
Semko, Mihail 133
Sheffield, HMS 116
Sicily 164, 184-7
Signal 6
Silk, Robert 8
Singapore 112-13, 124, 126-7
Slim, Bill 201
South Africa 76-7
Spanish Civil War 14, 15
Stalin, Josef 164
Stalingrad, Battle of 125, 130, 156-9, 164, 166-9
Stroop, Jürgen 171
submariners training 58
Sudentenland occupation 20-1
Sullivan brothers 153
Sword beach 212-17

T
Taranto raid 49
Tarawa, Battle of 165, 194-5
Teheran summit meeting 164
Tito, Marshall 165
Tobruk 87, 108-9, 124
"Torch" landings 124
Torgau 251

torpedo instruction 35
Tripoli 164
Tunisia 176-7

U
United States of America
  first draft 80
  nurses training 197
USA army
  black soldiers 138
  black troops 193
  in Britain 138-9
  Red Army 251
  Tunisia 177
USA Army Air Force (USAAF)
  332nd Fighter Group 218
  briefing 178
Usher, Corporal 269

V
VE Day 264-5
Victorious, HMS 140-1
Volkssturm troops 256-8

W
Warsaw rising 170-1, 200-1
West Virginia, USS 84-5
Western Desert 149, 160-1, 174-5
  Bardia 88-9
  Cauldron, The 111
  fitness training 150-1
  Operation Compass 49, 82-3, 90-1
  Operation Crusader 110
  training 82
  water 144-5
White, Harvey 185
Winter War 24-5, 40-1
Wojtyla, Karol 28
Wolf, Karl 65

Women's Auxiliary Air Force
  (WAAF) 75

Y
Yamethin 268
Yeremenko. Alexei 131
Yugoslavia 86, 165

Picture Acknowledgements

akg-images 31, 84, 104, 117, 120, 146, 164, 176, 182, 183, 193, 226, 241, 252, 250, 258, ullstein bild 12, 65, 132, 166, 201, 250, 255, 257;

alamy mary evans picture library 159, Pictorial Press 13;

associated newspapers 81;

australian war memorial museum 110, 153;

corbis 61, Bettmann 108, 118, 119, 187, 194, 206, 263, 282, Dmitri Baltermants Collection 102, 168, Hulton-Deutsch Collection 29, 37, 46, 58, 82, 108, 185, 202, 275, Yevgeny Khaldei 238;

getty images 10, 16, 19, 33, 40, 44, 59, 74, 83, 106, 107, 121, 133, 146, 154, 158, 167, 171, 184, 218, 244, 264, 277, 279, 280, A Hudson 44, Allan Jackson 251, David E Scherman/Time & Life Pictures 138, Davis 26, Frederic Lewis 170, George Rodger/Time & Life Pictures 128, George W Hales 36, Georgi Zelma 156, Heinrich Hoffmann/Time & Life Pictures 30, 55, Henry Guttmann 17, Imagno 25, John Florea/Time & Life Pictures 237, Leonard McCombe 236, Louis R Lowery/Time & Life Pictures 247, Popperfoto 24, 35, 122, 179, 240, R J Salmon 265, Ralph Morse/Time & Life Pictures 80, 152, Reg Speller 1, 53, Roger-Viollet 28, Time & Life Pictures 60, 62, 221, W Eugene Smith/Time & Life Pictures 229, 266;

imperial war museum 9, 39, 200, H1647 2, A12661 4, NA11626 6, E13374 7, FOX60432 8, HU32982 14, NYP22525 21, HU40002 32, HU75759 56, CH1406 70, CH7698 71, HU54418 72, LN6194 76, E3066E 87, E1579 88, E1553 89, E1611 90, E1636 90-1, E2172 92, MH5557 93, HU3947 96, HU39490 97, HU39518 98, E2535 99, E3625 101, RUS135 103, E5512 111, FE497 112, FE500 113, FE255 114, A6872 116, HU39698 124, HU31329 127, CF521 129, GM655 134, GM639 135, D4737 136, A9115 137, D17225 138, A8139 140, A11180 141, H22594 142, H22604 143, E8193 144, E11211 145, CM3958 148, E19145 148-9, E18761 150, E18762 151, E18557 160, CM4185 161, MH6345 162, AP258606 172, IB283 173, CM4698 174, E21337 175, AP261026 178, NA3435 180, NA3448 181, TA2142 188, IND1879 191, NYF18408 192, NA10325 196, NYT21628 197, NA15298 203, NA14990 204, NA14999 205, H39070 207, B5098 212, B5207 213, E48015 210, BU1181 212, AP26063 214, B5667 217, SE7910 232, SE2870 233, K7590 234, BU1159 235, SE2209 242, SE3640 243, HU22626 246, EA63141 253, RUS5138 256, CNA3401 257, BU5157 260, BU8609 274, MH24088 276, H42435 278;

magnum photos Robert Capa © 2001 By Cornell Capa 15, 177, 210, 225, Yosuke Yamahata/Collection Japanese 271;

mirrorpix 34, 42, 43, 48, 49, 50, 52, 51, 57, 67, 68, 69, 75, 77, 86, 94, 115, 186, 189, 190, 219, 213, 215, 222, 222-3, 224, 228, 261, 268, 268-9, 269, 281, 283, Central Press 38;

pa photos Deutsche Press-Agentur/DPA 100, 254;

peter newark's pictures 194, 20, 230, 267;

rex features 63, 78, 262, Alinari 270, CSU Archives/Everett Collection 211, Roger-Viollet 64, 66, 79, Sipa Press 198;

topfoto.co.uk Alinari 20, AP 18, Artmedia/HIP 226, RIA Novosti 105, 131, 169, Topham Picturepoint 54, 126, ullstein bild 22, 130.

Acknowledgements

The publishers would like to thank Michael Walsh for his meticulous work in researching captions and pictures at the Imperial War Museum and elsewhere. Thanks also to the staff at the Imperial War Museum for their help.

INDEXER Ian D. Crane
EDITOR Jo Wilson
PRODUCTION Caroline Alberti
CREATIVE DIRECTOR Geoff Fennell
PUBLISHER Mathew Clayton